THE
Archive Photographs
SERIES
AROUND
WHITBY

Seagulls are attracted to a bucketful of mussel shells emptied out on Haggerlythe in the 1950s.

THE
Archive Photographs
SERIES

AROUND

WHITBY

Compiled by
D.G. Sythes

TEMPUS

First published 1997
Copyright © D.G. Sythes and
the Whitby Literary and Philosophical Society, 1997

Tempus Publishing Limited
The Mill, Brimscombe Port,
Stroud, Gloucestershire, GL5 2QG

ISBN 0 7524 1025 3

Typesetting and origination by
Tempus Publishing Limited
Printed in Great Britain by
Midway Clark Printing, Wiltshire

*Royalties from this book are being donated to the photographic archive
of Whitby Museum for the conservation of the collection.*

The Dock End photographed around 1890 by Tom Watson. The masts and spars of the sailing ships stand out against the snow-covered east side. This part of Dock End was filled in during the 1930s. Today, where the foreground figures are carrying the cask, is the middle of the modern roundabout.

Contents

Acknowledgements

I would like to acknowledge the help and assistance I have received from Ernest Butler, without whose encouragement and help I would not even have attempted this book. I also thank Harold Brown, Sidney Barnett and Bernard Nelson, for helping me with their local knowledge. I thank the Keepers of Whitby Museum, Roger and Graham Pickles, and the Museum committee for permission to use the Museum's collection, of which I have the privilege of being curator. Thanks also to Bill Eglon Shaw and his son Mike, from the Sutcliffe Gallery in Flowergate, the Doran Brothers, and to John Tindale, for permission to use his photographs and his knowledge. Posthumous thanks are due to the past photographers of Whitby and District: Frank Meadow Sutcliffe, Tom Watson, Jack Vart, George Wallis, Hugh Lambert-Smith, and to the amateur photographers who, over the past hundred years, have given their photographs to the Whitby collection, some of which I have used. Not least, I thank my wife, long-suffering, who has had to put up with me while I was compiling this book.

A group of residents carry home kindling from a forage in Mulgrave Woods.

Introduction

Whitby is a town which has been lived in for thirteen hundred years, since the time of St Hilda who built the first Abbey. Whitby's population is roughly the same in the 1990s as it was in the 1790s, although perhaps spread out a little more. To get to, or leave Whitby, there are twenty miles of moors to cross, unless you leave by sea. It has always been like this, and one hopes it will always remain so, for it has foiled one of the twentieth century's greatest curses - urbanisation. This has bred a self- sufficient people, who steer by their own compass and who can be as infuriating in their cussedness as they are loveable. A favourite local saying is, 'there is a right way, a wrong way and the Whitby way'. Many make the mistake of thinking they are joking. The North Yorkshire Moors which surround the town are the largest area of heather left in the UK and one of the loveliest, and the most unspoilt.

Whitby and the surrounding area in medieval times was owned by the monasteries, as was much of the marginal land in Northern England. Whitby has always had a boom and bust economy. In early days this would have been dictated by the continental wars and the price of wool, but in later years it suffered from competition and its isolation.

The Whitby that people come to visit today is largely a Georgian town, although there are one or two medieval buildings remaining apart from the Abbey. Whitby during this period was a small but wealthy town because of whaling. Later the emergence of shipbuilding yards and the ancillary works of rope-making and sailcloth manufacture created much wealth and employment. Almost every business was associated, one way or another, with the sea. Whitby ships were prominent in the coal and Baltic trades, particularly after whaling transferred to Hull and Peterhead. During the nineteenth century the jet industry employed several hundred men, but declined rapidly after the 1870s. The villages of Staithes and Robin Hood's Bay owe their existence to fishing, and, in the eighteenth and nineteenth centuries, there were local alum workings at Boulby, Sandsend, Saltwick and the Peak.

During the nineteenth century, with the coming of the railway in the 1830s, the west side of the town was developed. The original plan by George Hudson, the so called 'Railway King', was to make Whitby a resort, not necessarily to rival its larger sister further south, Scarborough, but to complement it. George Hudson fell foul of the law, and his plans were completed by Sir George Elliott in a modified form. Since those days Whitby has changed year by year and, it must be said, not always for the better. The clearance of much of the old east side of Whitby in the 1960s in retrospect was somewhat severe. Many buildings were destroyed which should have been saved. Nobody at that time foresaw that tourism would be the financial backbone to the town's economy within thirty years, and that they were destroying what people would eventually pay to come and see.

For its size, Whitby must be one of the best visually documented towns in Britain. It has attracted over the years painters, many of them famous, such as Turner and the Staithes group of painters, as well as many bred in the town such as George Chambers, George Weatherill and his family. Print makers of the eighteenth century produced prints of the town, harbour, and Abbey by the hundred. Latterly, since the middle of the nineteenth century, many photographers have made a living in the town, and some of them were famous in their day both nationally and internationally.

The earliest photograph in this book is from 1862. The majority of the photographs are late Victorian and Edwardian. I have attempted to use as many photographs as possible from the large collection in the Whitby Museum which have not been published before. The Whitby Literary and Philosophical Society was established in 1823 and formed the Whitby Museum. Among its exhibits is a collection of fossils of international importance, along with the collection of scientific instruments by William Scoresby, a former whaling captain who became a member of the Royal Society. The Museum also houses a large photographic archive, much of it in negative form.

If our present generation has a duty, I feel it is to seek the narrow path between preservation and conservation of the past, and the commercial and social aspirations of the present and future.

D.G. Sythes,
Whitby, April 1997

The Australian-built replica of Captain Cook's *Endeavour*, berthed at Whitby in May 1997, within fifty yards of where the original *Endeavour* was built in 1765 as the collier *Earl of Pembroke*.

One
Around Whitby Harbour

Whitby Bridge from Spion Kop, 1996.

The River Esk and Whitby, from Larpool, c. 1900. The old dye factory is to the right and above that is the Whitehall Shipyard with a ship on the stocks. At the bottom left is the old gas works site.

One of the oldest surviving railway buildings in the world is the round weigh-house of the horse-drawn railway of the 1830s. It is now sadly vandalised.

Corner & Brown's timber yard at Dock End, with a brig alongside which was probably engaged in the Baltic timber trade. This photograph was taken on a camera club outing in 1906. To the right, Whitby Station is complete with its roof.

The Newcastle paddle-tug *Eddystone* ushers a brigantine into the berth occupied by the ship in the photograph above. The salmon coble in the foreground has her salmon licence number painted amidships.

A Scottish 'fifie' passes through the old Whitby Bridge which was built in 1835, and replaced by the present bridge in 1909. The carriageway to this old bridge was only just wide enough for a horse and cart. The white steam yacht in the background belonged to Sir George Elliott who completed the West Cliff estate after the bankruptcy of George Hudson, the 'Railway King'. He was also the local MP. The photograph was taken around 1905.

A barquentine lying in Dock End, with its sails loosened to a buntline for drying. She carries a figurehead. Her standing rigging is fast to outboard chain plates which would date her building from about the mid-nineteenth century. Just abaft the foremast can be seen the patent windmill used for pumping out the ship. Baltic timber ships were usually old and rather leaky.

This photograph, taken across the river from the east side in the 1860s, shows the topsail schooner *Barbara* built on the Tyne in 1826 and owned in Whitby from 1838. She was lost on Deal beach in 1907. It is the only known surviving photograph which shows a ship being built on the old Fishburn slipway, then owned by Hobkirk's. It was from this yard that Captain Cook's ships were originally launched. The ship is not named, but could be the *Revenge*, launched in 1863, which was the last ship built on the site, although a painting of her by Richard Weatherill does not show her with painted ports. Above her stern can be seen the masts of a sailing ship in Dock End. The shipyard buildings to the left were sold, with the yard, to the North Eastern Railway in the 1860s and were demolished to become the railway coal-yard.

A group of sailing vessels moored alongside New Quay in the early 1860s. The collier brig *Hazard* (left-hand ship) was built in Nova Scotia in 1823 and registered in Whitby in 1850. She stranded at Redcar on the 29 November 1880. The barquentine *Hopewell* (right-hand vessel) whose name can just be read on the taffrail aft, was built at Bo'ness in 1809. The vessel came on to the Whitby register in 1839. She had a long life, being broken up about 1890. The cobles in the foreground were of a slightly different type, having a pointed stern, and were known as 'mules'.

Compare this photograph with that above taken some forty or more years later. The building with the louvred upper windows, next to Collier's, now has the Angel Hotel vaults almost next to it. The big Scottish 'fifie' has been converted to steam, and the motor car has put in an appearance.

Regatta Day in Whitby, *c.* 1905. It has always been an important day for the town. The paddle steamer *Conqueror* was built at Piles yard at West Hartlepool in 1861 for the Dock and Railway Co., where she worked until 1902. After being sold she was a frequent visitor to Whitby around 1905 with other paddle steamers from Scarborough and Bridlington. The *Conqueror* survived for 73 years until 1934, when she was broken up.

Here, the five-masted schooner *Cap Palos* is alongside St Ann's Staith in 1919. She stranded at Robin Hood's Bay on her maiden voyage from Canada. She was refloated, and brought into Whitby where she remained for about a year. Eventually she was towed out for repair, but lost the tow in a gale as the tug was not strong enough to hold her. *Cap Palos* drifted and finally broke her back and sank north of Scarborough after only ever having made one voyage.

The Regatta swimming race off the Fish Pier, decorated with a banner of a well-known beverage, again around 1905. A large audience is seated in front of St Mary's church tower. The large old building above the advertisement for polish was the Weslyan chapel in Church Street, opened by Charles Wesley in 1763, and now demolished.

The paddle-tug *Emu* lies at the Coffee House End berth. She belonged to the Whitby and Robin Hood's Bay Steam Packet Co. A big Cornish lugger dries her sails while moored on the sands.

Pier Road sands in 1903, now dredged away for deeper draft vessels. The cobles lie bow to the river. In the background is the old 1835 Whitby Bridge with the buildings later known as 'Boots Corner'.

Pier Road sands in 1907. These sands were to disappear under the new fish quay in later years. The sands, as can be seen, were of a considerable width and ideal for careening a coble. This work is now done on Collier Hope sands.

A Cornish Lugger about 1890 with a Penzance registration number. The Cornishman was easily distinguished from the Scottish luggers by the long outrigger boom aft. These luggers followed the herring around the west coast, sailing through the Caledonian canal, and then down the east coast, finishing back in Cornwall by December.

The Scottish fisher-women at work along Pier Road at the turn of the century. They in turn followed their herring fleet around the coast. Behind the women is the shipping office of Harrowing's, now the Magpie Cafe. A little further on is the Nelson Flag public house, now demolished.

Five vessels came ashore between Upgang and the Piers during this storm in 1880. This photograph shows the remains of two fishing vessels abandoned and breaking up at the Battery in rough seas.

Whitby Harbour, pictured from St Mary's church, showing the herring fleet alongside Pier Road in the 1950s. The stone davits for the old lifeboat can be seen on Tate Hill pier.

Two photographs showing the building of the pier extensions which were completed just before the First World War. The steel framework on which the crane stands was referred to as the walking-man or iron man, and moved along as the work progressed. It was, of course, on rails.

The brig *Wellington* lies off Abraham's Bosom in the 1880s. Built at Prince Edward Island, Nova Scotia, she was owned by Marwood's, and was later lost off the South Pier at South Shields in 1892. In the background, on the skyline, can be seen the long building of the Ropery.

The west side of the upper harbour in 1877. To the right are the remains of a ship-building slipway, now part of a supermarket site. Above that is the open ground where the hospital was later to be built. The cottages to the right of the goods shed were pulled down in 1880.

This photograph, taken in 1871 from the bank near Esk Terrace, shows the old signal box, which was later moved up to the Bog Hall crossing. At the extreme right is part of the roof of the Esk Inn which was pulled down in 1904. The dry dock was the last surviving one on the west side and was owned by Turnbull's. It was later filled in, and the railway turntable built nearby. On Bell Island is the French schooner *Jean*. Esk Terrace (captain's walk) was the home of many Whitby ship masters. One has a flag staff with a yard and gaff outside his home.

A coble fishing for salmon in Sandsend Bay during the 1950s.

The *Crescent*, built in Guernsey in 1836. Here in 1876, and 40 years old, she is moored above the bridge drying her sails in calm conditions. St Michael's church and school are in the background.

Sailing vessels moored above the bridge around 1880. The old warehousing in Church Street was pulled down for road widening. The ships would probably have been laid up for winter, although the centre vessel appears to be laden. The steeple in the distance is that of the chapel at Larpool cemetery, which can no longer be seen because of trees.

This photograph, taken from an identical position as the one above around the same date, shows the entrance to Tin Ghaut, on the left, with St Michael's church and school. The paddler and other vessels are moored along Church Street, which includes Harker's jet workshops.

Whitehall Shipyard in the late 1860s in its heyday of wooden ship-building and repair. The ships are the *Mountaineer*, *Opal*, *Corunna*, and *George*.

An evocative photograph of the Fish Pier in 1938 with the *WY61 Easter Morn* alongside. At the far left of the picture is *WY1 Endeavour*.

The Scottish herring fleet in the lower harbour during the early 1950s, when the herring were plentiful after the six-year interval of the war. It was not to last, and by the mid 1960s fishing for herring on this scale had ended.

Fishermen of an earlier generation, around 1890, discharge their catch just below the bridge on New Quay. Note the variety of headwear.

A Lambert-Smith photograph, of the early 1960s, which shows the harbour from Marine Parade. The Lifeboat *Mary Ann Hepworth* is in her boathouse. The building behind the boathouse was shortly to be pulled down and replaced.

Another photograph by Lambert-Smith, from about the same date, taken below the steps at Marine Parade. Scottish herring boats from Inverness and Leith are moored alongside, with two Whitby cobles in the foreground.

The Lerwick-registered fishing boat *LK44 Margaret Reid*, alongside her compatriots at the Fish Quay on Pier Road, around 1960. She has unloaded her catch, which the Scots invariably did across the bow.

Salted herrings being shovelled, literally, into barrels on Pier Road in the late 1950s. It is a practice which would raise many eyebrows today.

Two
Around West Whitby

The old Whitby Bridge, taken from Spion Kop. This photograph was taken about 90 years before the picture on page nine.

Baxtergate, with the old Temperance Hall, left, which was replaced by the modern Midland Bank in 1905. The two bearded men in the foreground are outside Falkinbridge's Wine Vaults.

Falkinbridge's Wine Vaults. They were originally the Bridge Chapel, or Chapel of Ease, built in the fifteenth century and made redundant when St Ninian's was built and opened in 1778. It was adjacent to the gable end of what is now the entrance to the Midland Bank, Baxtergate.

The approach to the town in 1870 near the top of Prospect Hill. On the left is Hanover Terrace. At the bottom is Arundale House. On the skyline are the group of houses in Union Place, including Eskholm, and the Union Mill at Flowergate Cross.

The bottom of Prospect Hill, in the 1860s. Broomfield Terrace has not yet been built. The left-hand railings are of Hanover Terrace, and below is the corner of Arundale House. Also to be seen is the market garden which was later to become Pannett Park. Chubb Hill was not cut through until eighteen years later. The raised footpaths, of which there are several left in Whitby, are still there.

This drawing by an unnamed artist depicts Bagdale in the mid-nineteenth century. The Quaker burial ground is to the left. Broomfield Terrace was to be built in 1869, to the right of the man on horseback. The view of St John's church lancet windows, built in 1850, is today masked by St Hilda's church, built in 1867. It was between these dates that this drawing was executed .

Brunswick Street, formerly Scate Lane, in the 1880s, showing the Georgian Methodist church and school. They were pulled down for the building of the present Methodist church and the Brunswick Rooms in 1890/91, at a cost of £5,698.

Baxtergate in 1880 looking towards the Bridge. The tin bath which is hanging over Collier's doorway announces 'Baths for hire'. On the extreme right is the Belle Hotel, now a greengrocer's. Further along on the same side of the street is the Temperance Hall. On the left was Robinson's shop. The shop next to it repaired umbrellas. Both were demolished, and Talbot House and the present Yorkshire Bank were built on the site in 1888

The Belle Hotel in 1930. It was closed and converted to a shop and flats in 1935.

The 'Olde Ship Launch' around 1920, reputed to be one of the oldest buildings in Whitby. Dating from the fifteenth century, it is now the Smugglers' Cafe. The carving on the wall is believed to be part of the stern decoration of a captured smuggler caught and broken up in the 1830s. Behind the railings were the offices of the Whitby Waterworks Co.

Freeman Hardy and Willis' shoe shop at the end of Baxtergate in 1965. The business was consigned to history in 1996. It was one of the oldest businesses in Whitby, retailing from the same premises, since the First World War.

New Quay Road in 1908 showing the construction of the present Whitby Bridge. In the background, Collier & Sons, Ironmongers and Chandlers, occupy the building which was pulled down in the 1970s. On the extreme left the Midland Bank building is recognisable, with the back of Falkinbridge's Wine Vaults next to it. Across the river is Edgar Thornton's Sixpenny Bazaar and the Raffled Anchor Inn, both on Grape Lane. The young man with the bowler hat was the resident engineer for the building of the new bridge. The crane appears in an earlier picture at Scotch Head, being moved here to unload stone for the new bridge abutments.

The Plough Inn, Baxtergate, around 1920, before it was replaced by the modern 'Plough', built in line with Barclay's Bank and the old General Post Office.

Wellington Road in the 1930s. All the buildings in this photograph except Willisons the greengrocers, opposite the people seen crossing the road, were demolished to make way for the Co-op building in the 1930s. That business closed in 1996.

'Boots Corner' in 1939. It is remembered by many Whitby people, and is still referred to as Boots Corner, although the building was pulled down in 1974.

The same building when under the ownership of Robert Gray & Co. in the 1920s.

Boots Corner, photographed by John Tindale. The closed shops are waiting for demolition in 1974. The traffic warden is directing traffic at a very narrow corner, with two-way traffic across Whitby Bridge.

Baxtergate, also by J. Tindale. The new block being built in the 1960s was to include the new electricity show room in the nearest left-hand shop. Notice that almost all the buildings from St Ninian's are post-war, but follow the old medieval line. The older buildings largely remain on the right-hand side.

The Angel Hotel on New Quay Road in the 1920s. Compare this photograph with that on page fourteen. The Angel Hotel building is depicted in both photographs.

The end of Baxtergate and Victoria Square in the 1950s. The lower part of the building in the centre was converted to a shop, and was run by the Yorkshire School for the Blind. The building was pulled down for road widening in the 1960s.

Station Square in 1930. Paylor's is now the site of the public conveniences. Whitby and District Farmers was run by Tom Eves and is now incorporated into Trencher's Restaurant.

New Quay Garage on New Quay Road in the 1950s. The buildings are now part of Eves Garage

St Ann's Staith in the 1880s. The staith was, and still is, a licensed Customs quay for landing goods. Here the sloop *Republican* lies alongside, with a larger brig astern. The Buck Hotel site, at the far end, has been replaced by the Jolly Sailor. The large building in the centre was the old Whitby Brewing Company.

The shops along St Ann's Staith in the 1920s. To the left is the Red Lion public house, later to be demolished to build Woolworth's. The shop behind the lady was, until recently, Lawson's electrical shop. Next door to that is Collier's, the ironmongers, who had several businesses in the town.

The Jolly Sailor in the 1920s, before being redeveloped into the modern, present-day public house. The notice on the wall, on the left, states that the house could be opened on Market Days between 10 am and 11.30 am and 3 pm and 4 pm. Cyclists were also welcome.

Eglon's Neptune Fish Store, Haggersgate in 1958. It was one of the buildings in the block which succumbed to the bulldozer a few years later.

Haggersgate in the 1930s. The buildings on the left have been demolished for road widening. Those on the right have been restored. The far building, behind the lorry, was Harrowing's shipping office.

Bridge End, 1890. It was a favourite meeting place for locals, then as now, referred to by some as the University of Whitby. The drinking fountain presented to the town by Alderman Pannett is in its original position. It has now been moved closer to the railings and is minus the spherical gas lamp.

The Marine Hotel, around 1908. It was known locally as Coffee House End and was the site where fish were sold on the pavement and, like Bridge End, was a popular meeting place. Among the flags are a pair of sea-boots, fishing baskets and a 'gansey' - collection of decorations for a fisherman's wedding. Whitby new bridge is being constructed in the background.

Coffee House End fish sale, c. 1878. Some large cod have been laid out for sale. On the left are the paddle boxes of a steamer, which can be seen near the steps.

An Edwardian couple with their dog chat to one of the locals on Pier Road. The building behind the lady with the pram was the old Whitby Museum and Library and the ground floor was the Public Baths.

Pier Road, c. 1890. Again we can see the old museum building, now the Harbour Diner. Further along, near the boy, is Harrowing's shipping office, now the Magpie Cafe. Next door is the home of a local pilot.

Whitby has always attracted artists. Here an Edwardian artist sets up her easel near Coffee House End to paint a harbour scene. She has put on an apron, which suggests she is painting in oils. Apart from the inevitable small boy, she has attracted one admirer.

A summer scene along Pier Road around 1910. The fruit stall has a background of a lugger's tanned mainsail. Trade appears to be slack, as the young man has time to read. Behind him is a bollard with an iron top. One of these now stands outside the present Whitby Museum, but has rotted away to about a quarter of its size.

West Whitby, photographed in the 1890s by Joseph Vart ARPS. At the time the West Cliff estate was barely fifty years old. The Royal Hotel, and Kirby's, the long building facing the top of West Cliff, were the first to be constructed. Further along is the newly-built 1897 Metropole Hotel. Notice that there are no further buildings along the promenade until White Point is reached. To the left of White Point can be seen some white farm buildings, which were probably Stepney Farm, now The Parade. To the right and behind White Point is 'White House', Upgang. The Union Mill, minus its sails, can be seen. On the Battery, below the cliff, can be seen the former eighteenth century round powder house, and the Coastguard building with its short stumpy tower.

Pictured outside the harbour office in 1903, three elegant ladies, one with a pram, enjoy a walk along Pier Road.

Taken from almost the same spot, as the photograph above, on a post-war Bank Holiday in 1953. The crowd of people behind the ice-cream hut are listening to a brass band. The dredger *Esk* (the ratepayer's yacht) is moored mid-stream.

Pier Road end at the foot of the Khyber Pass in the 1930s. The stall was owned by a lady who sold lace.

Looking across the harbour from the photograph above, this view would be seen in 1898 of Tate Hill and the Henrietta Street area of Whitby, including the 199 church stairs, St Mary's church and the Abbey. Many of the buildings on Tate Hill have been demolished and replaced by modern post-war houses.

Three hardy holiday-makers are determined to enjoy themselves, despite a Whitby summer in the early 1960s.

The Bandstand outside the Spa in the 1890s. It was moved a few years later to a new position when the Spa Pavilion was built. It was later moved again to Scotch Head, where a bandstand remains today.

Two photographs taken by the Lythe photographer, Tom Watson, of a Temperance parade making its way up the Khyber Pass, in August 1898.

An Edwardian family walk along East Terrace in 1896, opposite what later became Kirby's Hotel.

Edwardians leave St Hilda's church, West Cliff, early in the century.

Milburn's Garage, John Street. They ran charabanc trips. The 'Karrier' bus at the kerb is one such vehicle. A trip to Hayburn Wyke along the coast was six shillings and to Egton Moors and Falling Foss two shillings. Next door was a tobacconist. Two doors up is the Masonic Hall.

The 'Elsinore' in the 1920s. During the early eighteenth century, it was the last house leaving or entering Whitby on the road up to Flowergate Cross. Here they sell Target Ales, which were brewed at Whitby Brewers on St Ann's Staith.

The top of Brunswick Street in 1895. The hoarding on the left marks the demolition of Stockton Walk the same year. All the other buildings, happily, remain. The hoarding for a 20-guinea piano was for a business in Skinner Street.

Isaac Stephenson's, a local plumber's shop housed in a Georgian building on Flowergate. In the 1920s it stood next to the old court building, now a solicitor's office. It was demolished earlier in the century and replaced by a modern building which is now a charity shop.

Hanson's Outfitters at the top of Flowergate with the entrance to Waterloo Place and Waterloo Hall on the extreme left. The hall was later converted into a cinema.

Flowergate in 1928. The bottom houses are being demolished to make way for Woolworth's store, which was opened a year later.

Flowergate. A photograph taken by Frank Sutcliffe in the 1890s, showing George Graham's ironmongery business, flanked by R.C. Cook's shoe shop, and W.R. Pearson, a jet jeweller. The Graham building was constructed in 1891. It is possible the photograph was a commissioned portrait for the business and the building.

A view of East Whitby, which cannot be seen today. It was taken at the bottom of Flowergate through the gap left by the demolished buildings prior to the building of Woolworth's in 1928/29.

Harrison's shop at the top of Golden Lion Bank. It was one of the buildings pulled down for the Woolworth's site.

The Congress Hall, taken from the top of Hudson Street in the late 1870s. The hall was moved to another site when St Hilda's, West Cliff, was built in the 1880s.

The Union Mill, with Union Place, including Eskholm, in the early 1880s. The Mill was erected in 1800 and traded for about eighty years. It was unusual in having five wands or sails. These were damaged and removed in the late 1880s when part of the roof was also lost

Union Mill taken from the top of John Street, around 1875, before the houses were built on Crescent Avenue. Notice that there are no buildings along Upgang Lane apart from Union Place.

The footpath and kissing gate which led from Flowergate Cross to Stakesby. The Union Mill is central, situated on the present site of Harrison's Garage. To the right are the 'New Buildings', now St Hilda's Terrace. The building on the extreme left is Arundale Howe. Just to the right of this house can be seen the long roof of Goodwill's Ropery. Chubb Hill does not appear to have been cut, which dates this picture before 1888.

Another Temperance parade, photographed by Tom Watson in the 1890s, at the top of Chubb Hill. The Union Mill has lost its sails and was shortly to be pulled down, leaving the lower mill building. It became a Drill Hall which survived until the mid 1930s. To the right is Tucker's Farm.

Skinner Street in the 1930s. The photograph was taken outside Botham's Bakery and Restaurant, which still occupies the same site. The street gives an appearance of being busier than it is today. One could even buy a piano here. It is also noticeable that the traffic was two-way. The shop opposite the parked bull-nosed Morris car was Cook's grocery store.

Jackson's Garage, in Silver Street, in the 1950s. They were the main Ford agents in Whitby. The white-haired gentleman on the right is the founder of the firm, George Jackson.

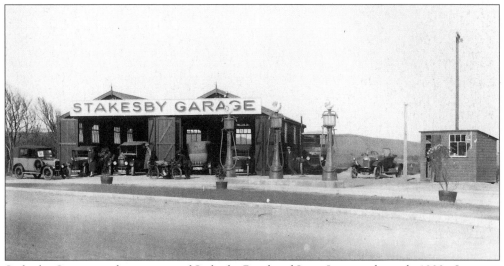

Stakesby Garage, at the junction of Stakesby Road and Love Lane in the early 1930s. It is now Arundale's Garage.

Upgang Lane at the crossroads of Station Avenue and Argyle Road in the mid 1930s.

Whitby whalebone arches brought back from the Greenland seas by the whaling fleet in the mid-nineteenth century. This pair were in Pannett Park, and were photographed by Hugh Lambert-Smith in the winter of 1946/47.

Whitby Gas Works. They were originally built in the 1860s, but are photographed here in the 1930s. Whitby was one of the first towns in Britain to have gas lighting, having whale-oil gas in 1825. Since that date several gas works have been built in and around the town. This gas plant was in operation until the advent of North Sea gas.

Almost next to the Gas Works, and below the railway viaduct, was this old shed made from whalebone jaws. It is here being pulled down in the 1930s. It was probably the source of the whalebone arches which appeared shortly afterwards in the district.

Two photographs taken in the 1920s of Lambert and Warters draper's shop in Fishburn Road. The area is referred to by local people as the 'Railway'. The shop is now the business premises of Walter Boyes the plumbers.

Three

Around East Whitby

No book on Whitby would be complete without at least one photograph of Whitby Abbey. This hitherto unpublished photograph was taken about the turn of the century and shows the Abbey much the same as it is today. It does not show the west door for comparison, which was later damaged during the bombardment of the east coast by the German High Seas Fleet in 1914. In any case the west door was largely restored. The jet seller is one of three ladies who ran this stall, Mesdames Walker, Middlemass, and Jackson. They occupied this place for many years during the summer months, carrying the wares up the 199 steps in the tin trunk under the table. The foreground stone wall was partly demolished by Revd Francis Haydn Willaims, a 'turbulent' priest who came to Whitby in 1888 to the Unitarian chapel, at the foot of Flowergate. One of the many things he campaigned against was that St Hilda's Abbey was surrounded by a high stone wall, which he alleged interfered with 'rights of way'. He and a few other like-minded individuals pulled it down. For this and other offences of failing to keep the peace he served a short time in prison. The displaced stone walling, behind the fence, was probably the remains left by the reverend gentleman as he passed this way shortly before the photograph was taken.

Haggerlythe in the 1950s. All the foreground in this photograph has slipped into the sea. The Spa Ladder leading to the East Pier is now prohibited access. Also demolished are the middle distant buildings on the sands by Tate Hill pier for post-war development

Donkeys being watered near Moreland Cottage, in Henrietta Street in the 1930s. They were then taken on to the sands for children's rides.

The Lady Cholmley School under construction in 1862. The school was built under the patronage of Lady Cholmley, wife of the Lord of the Manor, to replace the school on Haggerlythe, which was in danger of falling into the sea. Much of the stone of that school was re-used to build this one

The cobbled road on Tate Hill from Henrietta Street. All this has been redeveloped since the Second World War. Beyond the houses are the piers and the sands of Collier Hope, so named because the sailing colliers of yesteryear, during bad weather, would run in through the harbour entrance to beach themselves on the sands on a falling tide, which would leave them high and dry, but safe.

The Market outside the Old Town Hall in 1905.

A view of the Market Square, from the Old Town Hall in the 1930s.

A Frank Meadow Sutcliffe photograph of old Church Street which, happily, remains the same today 100 years later.

J.H. Wren outside his shop which was in the corner of Market Square, next to the Market Hall, now Burberry's.

Sandgate in 1880 by Frank M. Sutcliffe. The sign board of the 'Queen' is prominent. Johnson's butchers is on the left with its shop front open to the public. This area of Whitby was once a 'Shambles', where beasts were slaughtered.

The same street taken from outside the Queen's Hotel but looking the other way towards Market Square.

Bridge Street in the 1950s. Tyler's shoe shop is on the corner of Sandgate opposite the *Whitby Gazette* Office. At the top of the street is Wilcox's Store. All the buildings on the left were pulled down for road widening. As can be seen, it was a very narrow street.

A little further up Bridge Street than the photograph above, in about 1956. The shops on the left were by now all empty and awaiting demolition, which was done later that year.

Wilcox's Store, at the top of Bridge Street at the junction of Church Street in 1957. The store and the shop next door are closed and await the demolition men.

A John Tindale photograph taken a few months later than the one above. The replacement buildings are being erected on the Church Street site, after the clearance of the old dwellings, including Cappella House.

Grape Lane in 1950. The photographer's business at the entrance to Tin Ghaut had at one time been the Britannia Inn, from which the Ghaut took its name (t'inn Ghaut). Next to it is Captain Cook's House.

Picturesque 'Tin Ghaut'. Probably, next to Whitby Abbey, it was the most painted and photographed place in Whitby. Notwithstanding, it was pulled down with the other buildings in this photograph, except Cook's House. It is now part of the Church Street car park.

Alder's Waste Ghaut, later Virgin Pump Ghaut. It was the next yard to Tin Ghaut. The Virgin pump can be seen in this 1880s photograph. It was paid for by public subscription in 1827 and was the only source of running water for a large number of people. There is now nothing left of the Ghaut, or the pump.

Church Street, taken by J. Tindale, in 1970. On the right are the windows of the Quaker Meeting House. A little further along are some cottages with 'jetticks', the overhanging first floor timbers. The end cottage at the Grape Lane junction has been rebuilt completely 'as it was'. Behind the bus is St Michael's School, closed in 1970, and demolished shortly afterwards.

Church Street at the end of the last century. The building in the centre was demolished to make way for the Primitive Methodist chapel in Church Street in the early years of this century. The chapel itself has been closed for many years. The photograph is interesting for the Yorkshire sash windows in the buildings, which were a feature of Whitby Georgian architecture.

The old Imperial Public House in the 1950s. It has since been rebuilt and renamed. Next door, to the right, is the Primitive Methodist chapel which replaced the building in the photograph above.

Church Street in the 1860s, looking towards the bridge near the Seamen's Home. It illustrates the narrowness of the street for much of its length.

Photographed from almost the same place as above, in the 1920s, but looking along Church Street towards Green Lane.

Boulby Bank in the 1880s. The galleried houses, which were a feature of East Whitby, were built into the steep hillside, with the narrow cobbled passageways in between.

The same group of galleried houses as in the photograph above, which led from Church Street to the Ropery. It is reputed that twenty families lived in this block, with the outside privies to the right. They were demolished in the late 1950s.

The Gas Works on Church Street, built in 1837, are now incorporated into the Tyre Depot housed next door in the building with the doors.

Cook's blacksmith's shop near Boulby Bank in the 1930s. The circular plate on the ground, with the centre hole, was used for wheel-making and shrinking iron tyres on to cart wheels. The tyres were hammered on red hot and quickly doused with cold water, which shrank the tyre on to the wheel.

One of the many galleried east side yards, photographed early in the morning in the 1930s. These yards with their worn steps and cobbles were the favourite haunts for generations of artists.

The ropery on The Ropery in 1938. The original ropery on this site was built in 1721 and was 440 yards long. This Victorian brick-built replacement ropery is on the same site. It was finally pulled down after the Second World War and replaced by modern housing.

'Abraham's Bosom' and A.J. Bull's garage in Church Street, photographed by Doran's in 1930. Abraham's Bosom is the site of the Penny Hedge planting on Ascension Day Eve, a ceremony which has been carried out annually since medieval times. It was also, in former years, the only part of Church Street open to the river. The rest of the street was occupied by buildings as can be seen here. Bull's garage is now the Endeavour garage. The petrol pumps were on the other side of the street from the garage and sold Shell and National Benzole Mixture. Most of the buildings on that side of the street in this photograph have been retained. The chariot-type horse and cart were favoured by milkmen throughout the country. This may have been one of them. It will be noticed that beasts are being driven past the car, probably destined for the slaughterhouse in Market Square, now an artist's studio.

The dry-dock which was opposite Horner's Terrace, photographed after the First World War. The site is now the property of Northern Electric. The dock was one of two, which were almost adjacent to one another. They were built in 1734 and were filled in during the 1950s. The buildings to the right of the ship were the site of the electricity generating station.

This photograph was taken from the present Abbot's Road area in the 1890s. The other dry dock can be seen with the masts of the ship in the centre of the picture. The dry dock featured in the photograph above is where the crane jib is poking up a little further along. The foreground buildings are on Spital Bridge and Raft Yard

The Spital Bridge and California Beck area of Whitby in the 1870s, before the present Spital Bridge was driven through in 1876 on a line with the hand-cart in the middle foreground (compare this scene with the next photograph). Both dry docks are occupied by sailing ships, while another, with her topmasts and yards sent down, is either laid up, or waiting her turn for docking. In the foreground can be seen stacked timber. This area of California Beck was used as a timber pond in which ships in the Baltic timber trade deposited their cargoes. Just below the foreground footpath can be seen the roof of Abel Chapman's 1747 ropery. These roperies supplied the cordage required for the growing fleet of Whitby ships, especially in the whaling trade, and later in the coal and Baltic trades.

This photograph, taken by Joseph Vart, is of the same vista as the previous page about twenty-five years later. The line of Spital Bridge can be compared with the last photograph. The present bridge was driven through to replace the 1775 bridge which is still standing. The sailing ships have gone. The Whitehall Shipyard was by now building steamers such as the Turnbull ship on the left. A ship is under repair in the dry-dock with the crane. On the extreme right can be seen the long roof of the ropery. All along Church Street are the warehouses, which have now been cleared away for road widening, along with St Michael's church and school. In the foreground subtle alterations to the foreground buildings can be observed by comparison with the last picture. They were made when the new Spital Bridge was driven through.

This Weatherill painting shows the launching of the first steamship from the Whitehall yard in June 1871, called appropriately enough *Whitehall*. The white house, just above the ship, was the home of the yard's various owners and is also called Whitehall. At the top of the hill can be seen the steeple of the Cemetery Chapel with its house. The buildings at the bottom, extreme left, are those in the previous photographs of Spital Bridge. The building at the bottom, extreme right, was the Esk Inn which was demolished in 1905. It is noteworthy that a century later this scene is largely overgrown with trees and scrub, which would have been used for kindling in former times.

A 1900s view of Whitby which is also unobtainable today, taken by Sutcliffe at the end of Larpool Lane and Helredale Road. A whole estate has been erected on the site of the fields.

Four

Around and About
the Villages

The village of Ruswarp, about two miles from Whitby, has had a mill since medieval times. The Ruswarp Mill was built in 1752. This Sutcliffe photograph shows it before the fire of 1911 which largely destroyed it.

Ruswarp Old Bridge in the early 1920s. This bridge was washed away in a disastrous flash flood of October 1930, when many of the bridges along the Esk Valley were destroyed.

Ruswarp High Street, c. 1930. The street remains much the same today. The shop on the left is now the village Post Office and general store.

In 1931, floods struck again in Ruswarp, due to a prolonged period of heavy rain. On this occasion the lifeboat was taken from Whitby in order to rescue cottagers cut off by the fast-flowing water.

school

school House

A Humber car of the 1950s has just crossed Ruswarp new bridge, which replaced the bridge washed away by the floods of the 1930s. In the background is the Bridge Inn. The buildings on the left are the railway station and goods yard entrance. The Georgian house, which can be seen in a previous photograph, has just been demolished for road widening.

wrong.
It is the school I attended here
1950 - 56 ! So remember it

A few miles south of Whitby is Robin Hood's Bay, a former fishing community which has over the years bred generations of mariners who, up to a few years ago, could be found in any port in any part of the world. This classic view, taken by Hugh Lambert Smith in the 1950s, shows the sweep of the bay with the distant Ravenscar headland

Another classic view, taken about the same date, but at the bottom of Robin Hood's Bay. It shows the slipway with the Bay Hotel on the right.

The Dock and slipway at Robin Hood's Bay, at the end of the last century. The Coastguard House is on the right. Its large doors gave access to the life-saving apparatus (LSA), which included the breeches buoy and rocket-line throwing gear for ship-to-shore rescue, all pre-loaded on to a horse-drawn carriage. The LSA team consisted of local men trained by the Coastguard.

The Mariners Tavern, Robin Hood's Bay, is no longer licensed premises, but the scene has changed very little in the ninety years or so since this photograph was taken by Frank Sutcliffe.

One of the attractions of Robin Hood's Bay are the little narrow streets, which have never seen a motor-car or indeed any motorised vehicle. Many buildings which clung to the cliff side were lost through erosion, but there are still seventeenth and eighteenth century cottages left which have been lovingly restored to make 'Bay Town' unique to visit, or live in.

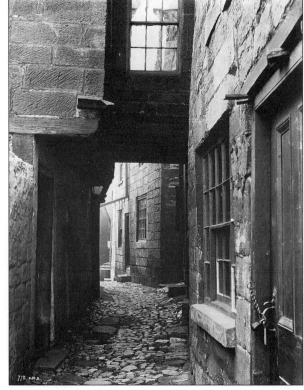

In this little gas-lit cobbled street the additions and alterations which have taken place in the buildings over the centuries can be seen by the inserted stone work of blocked doors and windows, along with the addition of Victorian bay-type windows.

Bay Bank, in the 1930s, with Barclay's Bank on the left. It is now a private shop. The chimney of the bakery can be seen in the centre of the picture, while a little to the right can be seen the notice on a gable end which reads 'Hardware Store'.

This Sutcliffe photograph of the early 1880s shows an identical view photographed from the same place about fifty years earlier. Barclay's Bank is here a humble cottage. The bottom shop is still a private dwelling. Horses had the unenviable job of hauling goods up and down this bank. Everything in Robin Hood's Bay had to go down or up this road. It still does.

Robin Hood's Bay from the beach looking towards the slipway. Another Sutcliffe photograph which is interesting to compare with today. The cliffs shown in this picture have been washed away with many of the houses. The same view today would show a considerable amount of concrete cliff stabilisation work which has stopped the Bay slipping into the sea.

Robin Hood's Bay from the south A view well-known to walkers of the coastal footpath. Most of the buildings in this Tom Watson photograph, taken in about the first decade of the century, are still standing. The photograph shows how the village clings to the sides of a steep narrow valley and has always been subject to landslip. There has been some additional building at the bank top from Edwardian times onward.

The annual Bay fair on the beach, photographed by Hugh P. Kendall in the 1920s. This fair was the highlight of the year, with horse-racing on the sands and the fairground rides on the slipway and beach.

St Stephen's church photographed in the 1890s by Tom Watson.

To the north of Whitby, across the bay, lies Sandsend, a village which occupies two small becks, joined by a frontage with two bridges which are open to vicious seas. This 1883 photograph by Tom Watson, taken from Tea-Pot Hill, shows the newly-completed railway station of the Whitby and Loftus Railway, which was formally opened the same year. Behind the station are the distorted and ravaged cliffs, remnants of the 200-year old industry, alum

mining. The remains of the alum works can be seen through the legs of the viaduct. Many of the other buildings in this photograph are still there, although the small group near the haystacks in the centre have disappeared. The viaduct, which was considered a monstrosity at the time of its erection, was in turn mourned by many on its demolition soon after the line was closed in 1958, a victim of Dr Beeching's axe.

This view of Sandsend Beck in the 1860s shows a little girl kneeling alongside the beck, roughly near the haystacks in the previous photograph. Although probably posed, as they had to be because of the exposure time, the photograph displays a tranquillity which must have been greatly disturbed twenty years later when the 'iron-horses' clattered over the viaduct as the forerunners of a noisier age.

Sandsend Alum Works. This photograph shows the remains as they were about 1920. The right-hand cottage and house were destroyed by a drifting sea mine during the Second World War. The buildings to the left were pulled down except for the front walls, which lead today to the large car park which now occupies the site of the former works.

East Row, Sandsend, in the 1880s. Most of the buildings in this picture are recognisable today, except for the bridge, which was washed away during a storm in 1910. Debris blocked the narrow arches and restricted the flow to breaking point. Behind the bridge can be seen the roof and small chimney of the Sandsend Brewery. Opposite the haystack on the right, were located the cement works and kiln.

Almost the same view as the photograph above, but also showing the viaduct. The white building is the Hart Inn which still retains its name and licence.

The main road at Sandsend after a storm in January 1902.

Another Tom Watson photograph taken in 1919. The cement works are at the extreme left. Roman cement was made from nodules which were found in the alum shale after that industry ceased working in the mid-nineteenth century.

This building at Sandsend which still stands, was photographed in 1889, when it was the cement works. Behind, to the right, can be seen part of the cement kiln.

A group of men standing outside the cement kiln. The unusual type of barrow was used to carry away the cement. Roman cement was, and still is, used for its ability to cure quickly under water, being invaluable for harbour and pier use where tidal waters dictate the drying time.

A 1930s No. 35 Leyland bus climbs up Lythe Bank on its way to Guisborough, Loftus, and Hinderwell.

One of a series of Sutcliffe photographs depicting the building of the Whitby to Loftus railway, taken in the late 1870s. This one shows the entrance to the newly-built Grinkle tunnel.

Midway between Whitby and Staithes lies the little village of Runswick Bay. Like Robin Hood's Bay, and to a lesser extent Staithes, it has had to contend with landslip and the ever-encroaching sea for most of its existence. These two photographs, taken in about the 1880s, show just how vulnerable the cottages were.

These fishermen's cottages can be identified by the impedimenta lying around outside, from lobster pots, to the carrying frame on the right which was used by two men to carry the nets and gear down the steep paths to the boats. Behind the lady with the bonnet can be seen a white umbrella with an artist working on a canvas. This area was at the time a favourite location for the Staithes Group of painters, of whom this artist was probably one.

The modern road would cut across this photograph of Runswick Bay today, otherwise there is much that can still be identified, not least the Royal Hotel, middle row right of centre.

Runswick Bay taken from the top of the cliff and looking towards Kettleness with the distorted cliffs created by alum working.

Runswick Bay landing and launch slip for the lifeboat. This is a print from the 1870s taken from a collodion glass negative.

Another view of the cottages of Runswick Bay taken by Tom Watson in the 1890s.

This photograph by Frank Sutcliffe shows how precarious some of these cottages were as they perched on the cliff side at Runswick Bay. The top group of cottages has an almost ecclesiastical look, as if it were a church and tower.

A group of 'gentry' playing about in a boat. The remarks of the children on the beach would doubtless have been interesting. The boat was owned by the Royal Hotel in the centre of the picture. The overdressed occupants were probably guests. A local lad has his place for'ard, the boatman holds the bow patiently, while the gentleman in the frock-coat pushes to get the boat further up on the beach in order that the lady may disembark with the decorum required of an Edwardian lady, and without getting her numerous petticoats wet. The Runswick children are hoping otherwise.

Staithes is the last of the trio of fishing villages. In this 1880s photograph, taken from the long-gone railway viaduct, Staithes Beck is shown meandering down to Cowbar Nab and the sea. It would be unusual to see so many boats so far up the beck today in the spot known locally as Low Coble Gardens. Also worthy of note are the neat and tidy vegetable plots on the beck side. The top house on the right was known as Badger Castle.

The cliffs and beach at Staithes at the point where the beck meets the North Sea. This photograph, also of 1880s vintage, is from the Cowbar Nab side. The small landing would be near the site of the Lifeboat slipway

Staithes Bridge. A very clear photograph of 1895, by Tom Watson. This old wooden bridge was the favourite place for the Staithes painters to pose the fisher-folk and the bridge appears in many of their paintings of around this date. The photograph shows some good examples of the

long narrow sailing cobles, built to launch and recover from a beach. Staithes was quite an important fishing village on the Yorkshire coast. Many of the buildings are still standing, which makes Staithes such a delightful place to visit.

Cowbar Nab in the 1890s. The fishermen here, as in Whitby, enjoy their clay pipes, and sou'-westers are the popular headgear. Notice the sixteen skips of baited long lines alongside the foreground coble. Women received 9d a line to bait these, including gathering the 'flithers' (mussels/limpets) to do so.

The same scene some fifty years later in the 1950s. The boats have gone, a sea defence wall has been erected to protect the Cod and Lobster area, and an outer breakwater has been built from the Nab, top right

This 1880s photograph by Frank Sutcliffe shows the cobles lined up below the mud bank which served as a harbour wall. Notice that what first appears to be a concrete wall is in fact a timber one. The erosion at this point shows why the improvements were made to the harbour walls in this area, which appear in the previous picture. The foreground shows a fishing family, together with the impedimenta of a fishing village, and some chickens.

The scene above is the left-hand side of this photograph taken from seaward about twenty-five years later by Tom Watson. The timber lath-type of harbour wall is now gradually being replaced by concrete sections. There are still a good number of sailing cobles on the beach. During the winter these would shelter in the Beck

A group of Staithes fishermen's cottages at the turn of the century, with groups of inhabitants in the distance. All the ladies are wearing the Staithes bonnet and the foreground boy is barefoot. Shoes were worn for school or not at all.

The main street at Staithes in the early 1930s, with Cowbar Nab in the distance. There appears to be some harbour work in progress; probably the outer breakwater is being built.

A Frank Sutcliffe photograph of Darnholm, with the stepping-stones, at the turn of the century.

Also by Frank Sutcliffe is this photograph of Beckhole, a village which is much the same today.

Saltwick Nab, c. 1890. The Nab is an outcrop of hard alum shale which lies at the north-west of Saltwick Bay. At the end of the Nab the line of breakers marks the site of the wreck of the hospital ship *Rohilla* in October 1914. Eighty-four lives were lost in a sea drama that lasted more than fifty hours.

Hawsker village, 1910. The Hare and Hounds public house is the right-hand building. Joseph R. Lacy was the licensee.

This is almost the last house after you leave Whitby on the Guisborough road, atop of Skelder. The New Inn at the end of last century was a country inn. Today it is a private house and remains the same except for the addition of the bottom windows, which are now Edwardian bay windows. The house is opposite the top exit of the Aislaby road.

For many years this building has been Sleights Post Office. It was, as can be seen, the former Country Cafe.

The temporary road bridge at Sleights after the bridge had been washed away during the 1930 floods.

During the 1880s many fine Georgian churches were rebuilt around Whitby during the so-called Gothic revival. Sleights church was one that was pulled down, to be replaced by a church which had to look medieval according to the fashion of the day.

114

Five

People

Fishermen of a much earlier generation on Tate Hill pier. It would be interesting to know what they are looking at, or for.

Two small boys who lived high up in one of the many yards and ghauts, such as The Cragg on the West Side, and Boulby on the East Side.

This posed photograph shows one of the galleried cottages of a Whitby yard, probably Wilson's Yard. The woman's basket is resting on the public bakehouse oven.

A boy models the 'truant's clog' which was used at the Mount School in 1874. The clog is now in Whitby Museum.

Staithes women-folk helping their men to beach a coble in the 1880s. This was a usual occurrence when most of the male population of the village were at sea.

The printers of Horne's *Whitby Gazette* in 1929.

Two fishermen repairing their nets along the fish quay at Pier Road.

The ladies and gentlemen of the Brunswick Methodist church choir, photographed in 1914 by Tom Watson.

Watching other people work is an occupation everyone enjoys sometime or another. In this 1950s photograph a group of visitors watch as 'Mucka' George Winspear makes a net along Pier Road, opposite the Pier Hotel.

Further along, about the same date, three girls watch an artist on the West Pier.

Whitby Beach just below the Battery in the 1950s, before the mass exodus to guaranteed sunnier climes.

An entertainer performs on the plinth of one of the Powder Houses on the Battery in the 1950s.

A Scout Troop in 1920. The photograph was taken outside the Scout hut which stood on the site of the present bungalows on Bobby's Bank. The long building in the background was the railway dray-horse stable.

A Gang Show, which appears to have been held in the St John Ambulance Hall in the 1930s. It proves the strength of the Scout movement in Whitby in those days.

This charming photograph was taken by a Birmingham photographer in the 1930s for a competition, which it won. It shows the blind man Billy Poyer, who for thirty years in the summer sat at the foot of the steps on the Khyber Pass, which lead up to the Cook monument (depicted in the earlier photographs of the Temperance parade). He knitted socks most of the time, and his dog was a great favourite of children. In the winter he sat on the steps of Leeds Town Hall.

On 22 September 1914, three cruisers *Crecy*, *Hogue*, and *Aboukir* were sunk by submarine in the North Sea with great loss of life. Thinking one of them had been mined, the other two stopped to pick up survivors, and were in turn torpedoed. This was the first instance of the sinking of a ship without warning by U-boat. Casualties included many reservists recently called to the colours from Whitby. It was not known for certain until 1919 that the ships had indeed been sunk by U-boat (U-9. Lt. Otto Weddigen) and not mined as had been thought at the time. This photograph is of the Whitby survivors.

The lady sitting on the left with her family is Mrs Mary Roberts, who served as stewardess aboard the ill-fated ships *Titanic* (sunk in April 1912) and the *Rohilla* (sunk in October 1914). She survived both disasters.

A group of Victorian ladies enjoying themselves in a boat, on the upper reaches of the river Esk just below the dye factory. The laughing lady in the bow was Miss Bessie Wiseman who was a temperance preacher. She was married late in life to Mr Bell and they lived in a cottage on Castle Road.

Irene Sutcliffe, daughter of the photographer Frank Sutcliffe, who appeared in many early photographs taken at Ewe Cote, and Carr Hill Lane, during her childhood.

If ever you have stood under Whitby Viaduct, and wondered at the skill of the 'brickies' who built it, here they are. The brickies are the ones holding their trowels like a badge of office. The others are the hod carriers who carried every brick in the construction - one million of them. The viaduct was built in 1884, taking eighteen months to construct. That is about half the time of the construction of the present high-level bridge ninety years later.

Tom Watson of Lythe (1863-1957). Tom Watson was ten years younger than Frank Sutcliffe. Their careers ran parallel in Whitby. Although Tom Watson has perhaps been overshadowed by Sutcliffe in the past, Watson's photographs are renowned for their detail and clarity which, from an historical point of view, are unsurpassed. He has in recent years been brought to the attention of a wider public by the publications of Dr G. Richardson, FRPS.

George Wallis, photographed by Tom Watson outside his house at Sleights. Not much is known about Wallis, except that he took over the studio of John Stonehouse, at Khyber House, now Streonshalh House on the Khyber Pass, sometime in the 1880s.

The eminent Victorian photographer, Frank Meadow Sutcliffe (1853-1941). He is photographed here in the old Whitby Museum on Pier Road prior to its move to Pannett Park. FMS, as he was known, was for many years secretary to the Whitby Literary and Philosophical Society, which runs Whitby Museum. The Sutcliffe Gallery on Flowergate has a large collection of Sutcliffe photographs on permanent display

Frank Meadow Sutcliffe's father Thomas was a Leeds watercolourist, who brought his family to live in Whitby during the 1880s. This painting by Thomas, executed in the 1850s while they were on holiday, shows his family in the foreground, with Frank Sutcliffe as a little boy at his mother's knee, and his brothers and sisters.